DISCIPLINE

A Play

by

Gerard Bianco

iUniverse, Inc.
Bloomington

Discipline
A Play

iUniverse books may be ordered through booksellers or by contacting:

iUniverse
1663 Liberty Drive
Bloomington, IN 47403
www.iuniverse.com
1-800-Authors (1-800-288-4677)

ISBN: 978-1-4620-7022-0 (sc)
ISBN: 978-1-4620-7023-7 (e)

Printed in the United States of America

iUniverse rev. date: 12/22/2011

For V,
my lovely daughter.
I miss you.

Acknowledgments

I would like to thank family and friends who read the manuscript during its infancy, adding advice along the way.

Special thanks to Rhonda Farnham Photography for making me look good in the author photo.

Thank you to Kathleen Egan, Claudia Dricot, and Elizabeth Isele for their editorial expertise.

Finally, I'd like to thank my son, Gerard Jr., for his assistance and inspiration while developing the play and my companion and best friend, Caterina, for her patience and understanding while I worked on the manuscript.

DISCIPLINE

A Play

Cast of Characters

HAROLD JENKINS, forty years old

LILLY, forty years old

FRUSTRATO, forty years old

POLICEMAN, fifty years old, one of New York City's finest

Place

The seventeenth-floor apartment of HAROLD JENKINS in the Chelsea neighborhood of Manhattan.

Time

Act One: Summer, 1:00 a.m.

Act Two: The next night, 11:30 p.m.

Act One

(After midnight in the one-bedroom apartment of HAROLD
JENKINS. *Downstage right is a dining room where two
chairs sit opposite each other at a small, rectangular
table. A plate with crumbs, a glass with some soda, and a
crumpled napkin are at one end of the table. An entrance
door is off the dining room. Behind the dining room is a
small, windowless, U-shaped kitchen. The stove is in the
center of the U, facing the audience. Downstage center is
a small living room, sparsely furnished. Downstage left is
a bedroom. In the bedroom, the foot of the bed faces the
audience. A nightstand with a lamp and telephone sits
on the left side of the bed; a dresser is on the right side.
Next to the dresser is a window, which looks out onto
Eighteenth Street. Upstage center is a bathroom door.*

HAROLD *and* LILLY *are in the bedroom, sitting up in
bed. The bedroom door is closed. The nightstand lamp
is lit. The rest of the stage is dark.* HAROLD, *lamp side, is
wearing pajamas and looking at the photos in a* Playboy
magazine. LILLY *is wearing a sexy Victoria Secret
nightgown. She sits, doing nothing.)*

HAROLD

(Looking at the magazine, he pauses, looks at LILLY. *She looks at him. He looks back at the magazine, then again at her. They repeat this two more times.)* I find that no two nipples are alike—even on the same person.

LILLY

It's not polite to compare them.

HAROLD

I wouldn't know why.

LILLY

I wouldn't think you would, so I'll tell you.

HAROLD

I knew you would.

LILLY

It's not polite to compare nipples because it shows disrespect for either one or the other. Besides, it's rude to move your head between the two as if you were at a tennis match. *(She moves her head from side to side.)* The correct way to look at nipples is to stare straight ahead, without showing favoritism of any sort. *(She illustrates by staring straight ahead.)*

HAROLD

I had no idea there was a correct way to look at nipples.

LILLY

There's a correct way to do everything; not that I would ever expect *you* to understand that.

HAROLD

What are you saying? Are you implying that I do not do things correctly?

LILLY

Did a light just go on?

HAROLD

Why, I do lots of things correctly.

LILLY

Really? Name one.

HAROLD

(Thinking) I shave. I get up in the morning and I shave, correctly.

LILLY

No you don't.

HAROLD

Don't be absurd, of course I do. I've been shaving my whole life. I shave correctly.

LILLY

I've watched you shave. You shave like a moron.

HAROLD

Why, that's news. And how does a moron shave?

LILLY

You shave your entire face in one direction—down. *(She illustrates on her face.)*

HAROLD

So, what's your point?

LILLY

There are places you can't reach by shaving down. *(She illustrates, puffing out her cheek and then her upper lip.)* You should shave up and down. Also, if you shave in both directions, you won't cut yourself the way you normally do.

HAROLD

When were you going to mention this?

LILLY

I've been meaning to.

HAROLD

I could have saved quarts of blood had you said something sooner.

LILLY

Sorry, slipped my mind.

HAROLD

I used to do things correctly. Now, for some reason …

LILLY

That was before.

HAROLD

If only I could do things like I used to. I can't seem to
remember things—things we've discussed. Nothing is
achieved without great difficulty these days.

LILLY

You can't go backwards, you know.

HAROLD

I bet it's the pills.

LILLY

Are you certain it's only the pills?

HAROLD

It's the pills, I tell you.

LILLY

If you have to blame something, it might as well be the
pills.

HAROLD

Why must I take the pills?

LILLY

They say you need them.

HAROLD

But who are they?

LILLY

They've always been there. It's only now that they've come to the forefront.

HAROLD

I wish to hell they'd go back to where they came from.

LILLY

If they won't go back, why don't you move forward?

HAROLD

(Contemplating) Which way *is* forward? (*He pauses, then looks once again at the magazine.*) Have you ever noticed that some nipples take on the shape of other objects?

LILLY

I can't say that I have.

HAROLD

They most definitely do. Sometimes they look like little lily pads, while other times they look like anthills. Here, you see—look at this one. *(He shoves the magazine in her direction. She looks closely.)* Wouldn't you expect a little ant to pop out of that at any moment? Oh, and here—here's one that looks like a doorbell. You see that? *(He presses the magazine with his thumb. Then, in a singsong voice.)* Ding-dong! Ding-dong! *(He smiles at her.)* Ding-dong!

LILLY

You're an idiot.

HAROLD

Lilly, I think tonight is a good time for us to do it.

LILLY

You've been looking at too many doorbells, Harold.

HAROLD

I think tonight is a *very* good time for us to do it.

LILLY

You think anytime is a good time to do it.

HAROLD

I think tonight is a good time to do it because we didn't do it last night.

LILLY

That's right, Harold; we didn't do it last night. You did it alone.

HAROLD

It doesn't count when I do it alone.

LILLY

It counts double when you do it alone.

HAROLD

Double? Since when?

LILLY

Since you do it almost every night, alone.

HAROLD

Come on, Lilly—what do you say? Let's do it, shall we?

LILLY

(In a sexy voice, smiling, reaching up, and holding her breasts.) You like doorbells, don't you, Harold?

HAROLD

You know I do.

LILLY

You like looking at them?

HAROLD

Without a doubt.

LILLY

Touching them?

HAROLD

Utterly.

LILLY

Squeezing them?

HAROLD

Enormously.

LILLY

Kissing them?

HAROLD

Totally.

LILLY

Is that why you buy these magazines?

HAROLD

I guess you could say that.

LILLY

Would you like to see *my* doorbells, Harold? Would you like to ring them?

HAROLD

Absolutely.

LILLY

That would really excite you, wouldn't it?

HAROLD

Uh-huh!

LILLY

Would it excite you?

HAROLD

Uh-huh!

LILLY

It would.

HAROLD

Uh-huh!

LILLY

Wouldn't it?

HAROLD

Uh-huh!

LILLY

It *would* really excite you, *wouldn't* it?

HAROLD

Uh-huh!

LILLY

I'm wondering how *would it* and *wouldn't it* can mean the same thing.

HAROLD

I don't get it.

LILLY

You answered uh-huh to both. I said, "Would it?" You said, "Uh-huh." Then I said, "Wouldn't it?" and you said, "Uh-huh." I'm thinking it should be either *would* or *wouldn't*, but not both. Get my drift?

HAROLD

I'm lost.

LILLY

It wouldn't be the first time. *(Pauses.)* What were we talking about?

HAROLD

Doorbells.

LILLY

Oh, right. They *would* really excite you, *wouldn't* they?

HAROLD

Completely. Let's do it.

LILLY

There I go again! You see that?

HAROLD

See what?

LILLY

I used both of them in the same sentence, and it made perfect sense.

HAROLD

I still don't get it.

LILLY

I'm not surprised. Where were we?

HAROLD

Doorbells.

LILLY

(With feeling, touching her breasts.) Oh, I want to, Harold ... I want to do it so badly—you know I do—but I can't.

HAROLD

Why not?

LILLY

I have my period.

HAROLD

You don't get a period, Lilly.

LILLY

Oh yes I do, Harold. It comes right after NO FUCKING WAY—IT AIN'T HAPPENING TONIGHT, PERIOD!

HAROLD

You know what you are, Lilly. You're a ... a DT.

LILLY

Ah-ha! There's a new one. A DT, eh? And what is a DT, if I might ask?

HAROLD

DT stands for "dick teaser." You're a dick teaser, Lilly. That's exactly what you are. A big dick teaser. Capital *D*, capital *T*. DT—dick teaser! You wear sexy nightgowns with your doorbells hanging out, and then when I get excited and I want to touch them, you push me away. That's what a DT does, Lilly. They tease and push away. Tease and push away.

LILLY

Thank you, Harold, for that insightful explanation. Now when I go to bingo on Friday night over at Our Lady of the—whatever—Holy Rollers—I can tell Sister Superior that I'm a dick teaser. I think I'll ask her advice on the subject. I'll say, "Excuse me, Sister, but I am a big dick teaser. Have you any advice for me this evening?" She will look at me with suspicion to see if my heart is in the right place, and when she realizes I want to change my dick-teasing ways, she'll say, "Shame on you for holding out on the poor boy. Why not give him a little nooky tonight, my child?"

HAROLD

Yes! Exactly right! You nailed it. She'll sympathize with me.

LILLY

You think so?

HAROLD

Absolutely.

LILLY

She's a woman of the cloth, you know?

HAROLD

They have feelings too.

LILLY

Yes, but they have them in all the wrong places.

HAROLD

It doesn't matter; she'd tell you to go for it.

LILLY

Only one problem.

HAROLD

What's that?

LILLY

There is something that Sister Superior doesn't know about you that I do.

HAROLD

Which is?

LILLY

That you're always horny! Forget about this nightgown; you'd want to do it no matter what I was wearing. I could be dressed in a fucking Eskimo's parka wearing burlap panties with the goddamn covers pulled up over my head, but as long as I had one little naked fucking pinky toe sticking out of these covers *(She sticks her foot out from under the covers.)* you'd be as horny as a dog in heat.

HAROLD

That's because you have sexy pinky toes, Lilly. You have sexy everything, and I would love some of that sexiness right now.

LILLY

Get a grip, Harold, and I don't mean on that thing of yours. Now turn out the light. We'll talk about your behavior in the morning.

HAROLD

Okay, Lilly, I'll turn out the light, but one day, you'll see … I won't need you. I'll have someone else who will take care of me. And then watch out. It will be like old times again. That's right. YIPADEE-YOH-KIYA. RIDE 'EM HIGH, COWBOY! HEE-HAW! *(He moves as if riding a horse, one hand on the reins, the other waving a lasso in the air.)* HEE-HAW! *(Pauses, looks at* LILLY.*)*

LILLY

Are you totally insane? Yes, of course you are. Why am I asking? You've lost your fucking mind completely. Have you forgotten that's the same behavior that made them lock you up? Do you want a repeat of that pleasant experience? Jesus, Harold, wake up! Have some discipline! Take one of those yellow pills in the morning and you won't feel so fucking horny. Discipline, remember? We have to show them that we can make it on our own, otherwise they will separate us. They're just waiting for any old excuse to do it. So please ... discipline. Okay? You'll see, we're doing the right thing. You know I'm right. I'm *always* right.

HAROLD

Yes, Lilly, I know you're always right. I hate it that you're always right. Can't you ever be wrong—just once? To err is human, you know.

LILLY

That's right, Harold, and you're the most human person I know. Now turn out that goddamn light and go to sleep. (*Turning away from him and pulling the covers over her shoulder.*) Sweet dreams, Harold.

HAROLD

(*Under his breath*) Yeah, sweet dreams, my ass.

LILLY

What was that?

HAROLD

I said, "Good night, Lilly, sweet dreams to you, too."
(Pauses.) Say, Lilly? I need to know something.

LILLY

Harold!

HAROLD

Sorry, Lilly, I have no alternative. I have to ask this. Why
do you use such foul language? Why do you curse so?

LILLY

One of us should, don't you think?

HAROLD

I suppose you're right. I'm glad it's not me. You're
much better at it then I am. It's amazing, when you use
foul language it sounds almost like … poetry. Me, on
the other hand … I can never remember which word
goes first. But you, Lilly, you have such an enormous
command of the language. I truly admire that discipline.
It's admirable. I am in awe. Really … *in awe* … in awe!
(Then, overly sweet.) Good night, sweet Lilly. (HAROLD
turns off the light. The stage goes completely dark.)

LILLY

Harold, I don't care how many compliments you throw
my way this evening, I'm not letting you wank off
tonight, and that's final!

HAROLD

I don't *wank off.* *(Pauses.)* I relieve my anxiety.

LILLY

You relieve your anxiety by wanking off! Tonight, however, you will have discipline—am I right? *(After a moment.)* Harold! Get your hand off that thing. Discipline, remember?

HAROLD

Okay, okay. There, is that better?

LILLY

No! Get your fucking hand off my doorbell!

HAROLD

All right! All right! Good night!

(After a few moments, we hear sniffling from somewhere outside the bedroom. HAROLD *turns on the lamp and sits up.* LILLY *is sleeping on her side, her back toward* HAROLD.*)*

HAROLD

(Slightly above a whisper.) Lilly! Did you hear that? *(No response.)* Lilly? Are you awake?

LILLY

(Turning toward HAROLD, *groaning.)* I was sleeping. Couldn't you see that I was sleeping? Can't you ever give it a rest? What is it this time?

HAROLD

I heard something—out there—and I think it's—

LILLY

Wait! Don't tell me! I don't want to know. Whatever it is, let's pretend it's not happening, okay? It'll go away, I promise.

HAROLD

Shhh, keep your voice down! I heard a strange noise … listen … *(Sniffling.)* Uh-huh … uh-huh—yes, there it is again … Did you hear that? Oh my God, Lilly, I think there's someone in the apartment!

LILLY

I didn't hear a thing, Harold, and if you did, I'm certain there's a perfectly good explanation for it. So just quit, okay? We've got to get up early. We have an appointment with Dr. Carney tomorrow. Have you forgotten? We have no time for nonsense. (LILLY *turns her back on* HAROLD *and pulls the blankets around her neck.* HAROLD *continues to sit up, waiting for the noise to repeat. After a minute, when nothing happens …)*

HAROLD

I guess you're right. It was probably nothing. *Damn* I hate it that you're always right! Just one time I want you to be wrong, okay? Just one time. Is that asking too much? Just one time! (HAROLD *turns off the light. After a few moments we hear the sniffling noise again.* HAROLD *turns on the light, then continues in an urgent whisper.*) Okay, that's it! Lilly, I swear, this time I heard something. Someone is definitely out there! (LILLY *ignores him.*) Lilly? Lilly? (LILLY *continues to ignore him.*) Lilly! I think we should check out the noise, don't you? Lilly? Don't you think we should check out the noise? You know ... see what it is? (LILLY *continues to ignore him.*) Lilly, I *said* we should go out there and see what that noise is. Are you coming? (HAROLD *twists his mouth in anger, throws off the covers and slips out of bed. His feet sink into beige-colored, sheepskin-lined slippers. He reaches for his robe hanging behind the door on a hook. It is a white, fluffy terrycloth robe with a big H monogrammed in red on the breast pocket.*) Okay, I'm going out there now. (*Pauses, looking at* LILLY.) I said, I'm going to go out there now and check to see what the noise is, in case you want to come with me. (*No response.*) Okay then, here I go. Just me ... by myself ... checking ... without you. Just one thing before I go: if I don't come back, tell Dr. Carney that he and his pills have ruined my life.

(HAROLD *turns off the lamp, opens the bedroom door, and flicks a wall switch, which turns on a small lava lamp in the living room. The rest of the apartment is still in darkness. He stops and listens, hoping to pinpoint the location of the sound. It remains quiet. He turns and looks back into the bedroom.* HAROLD *closes the door and tiptoes into the living room. He peers into the darkened corners. He sees nothing. He hears the noise again. It's coming from the kitchen. Slowly, he moves toward the sound. Cautiously, he peers into the kitchen and flicks the light on. To his surprise,* FRUSTRATO *is crouching on the stove.* HAROLD *brings his hand to his mouth. The man is in profile, staring straight ahead, sniffling. He is extremely thin—nearly emaciated—with a long, skinny nose. In the soft light, his high cheek bones cast deep, dark shadows on his cheeks. He is dressed in a black-and-white, horizontal-striped T-shirt, tight black pants, and black slippers. A black stocking cap sits on his head and contrasts with his gaunt face, which is white—so white it appears as if he is wearing makeup.* HAROLD *watches in stunned silence. The man turns toward* HAROLD.)

FRUSTRATO

(Sniffling.) I don't want to be here! Do you hear me? I said I don't want to be here!

(HAROLD *reacts quickly. He shuts the light in the kitchen and runs as fast as his feet will take him back towards the bedroom. He flicks off the living room light and runs into the bedroom. He slams the door and turns on his lamp.* LILLY *sits up with a jolt. With trembling hands,* HAROLD *locks the door.)*

LILLY

What! What is it?

HAROLD

(His back and palms against the door, excited and out of breath.) Oh my God, Lilly! There's a man on our stove!

LILLY

What?

HAROLD

(Breathing heavily, he places a hand over his chest.) Oh, my God, my heart is pounding like a jackhammer. *(He pretends he's using a jackhammer.)* BBBBBBBBBBBBRRRRRRRRRRRRRR. *(Puts his hand back on his heart.)* Geez, I hope I don't have a heart attack.

LILLY

Harold, what the fuck is going on?

HAROLD

Did you hear me? There's a man on our stove! Quickly, do something! Call the police!

LILLY

(Sitting with her arms across her chest and looking at HAROLD *in disgust.)* You're a dimwit. First you wake me up from a sound sleep with complaints of noises, and now you pretend to see someone just to prove you're not crazy. But you know something? You are crazy, Harold. You're as crazy as a loon. Crazier, sometimes. *A man on our stove.* So what's he doing, peeling fucking potatoes?

HAROLD

Lilly, I swear to you, there is a man out there, and he's on our stove! Go see for yourself if you don't believe me. Only don't say I didn't warn you.

LILLY

Do you think I'm an idiot? Do you think I'm going to search this apartment in the middle of the fucking night looking for someone who is not there just to prove you're crazy? I don't need to do that; all I need to do is look at you to see that you're a certified nut case. *There is no one there!* Now get back into bed and go to sleep!

HAROLD

That's okay, Lilly. I'm glad you're not going out there. You want to know why? Protection!

LILLY

Protection?

HAROLD

Yes, that's right. Protection. In here, I can protect you. Out there, who knows what would happen to you. Who knows what a guy like that might do to you if you go out there. I can only imagine. Why, I bet he'd sneak up behind you, grab you by your doorbells, and throw you down. Then he'd strip off all your clothes and have his way with you—over and over. Over ... and over ... and over ...over ... and over—

LILLY

All right, Harold! That's enough! You've had your fun. Now get back into bed.

HAROLD

Doubt me if you want, Lilly, but I swear to you, there's a man out there, and I'm going to do something about it.

LILLY

(Panicking.) What? What are you going to do?

HAROLD

I'm going to call the police—that's what I'm going to do.

LILLY

Harold, you're not calling the police!

HAROLD

I have to, Lilly. Don't you understand? There's a strange man on our stove!

(HAROLD *picks up the phone.*)

LILLY

Don't do it, Harold! Please, do not call the police!

(HAROLD *presses 9-1-1.*)

I said don't do it! They'll think you're crazy. You know what could happen …

HAROLD

No one is going to think I'm crazy, because when they get here, they'll see that … Oh, hello. Police? Good. This is Harold Jenkins at 219 West Eighteenth Street, apartment 17B … No … not Seventeenth Street, Eighteenth Street; 17B is the number of the apartment. No, not nineteen … Yes, yes, I said nineteen but nineteen is in the number of the address … at the beginning … before the other numbers … except two. Nineteen comes after the two. What? No, not 192, it's the other way … Wait a minute! Will you just listen to me for a second! There is a strange man in my apartment! … No, no one is hurt … No, I don't know what he's doing. *How the hell should I know what he's doing?* … No, I'm not shouting … No, sorry … What? … Yes, of course I'm in danger. I don't know what this guy is capable of ... I'm in my bedroom and the door is locked. Can you send someone over right away? ... You can? ... Splendid ... Yes, of course I'll be here. Where am I going to go? Food shopping? It's the middle of the night fucking.

(LILLY *uses her hands to show that he should have reversed the curse word. He grimaces when he realizes he said the words backward.*)

HAROLD

Yeah, yeah ... okay ... No, I'm sorry ... Yes, you're right, I shouldn't have used that language, I'm not good at it ... Okay, yes, I'll stay locked in the bedroom until the police arrive, I promise ... *No*, I said *I'm not going anywhere* ... Yes, I'll repeat my address—listen this time. It's 219 West Eighteenth Street. Apartment 17B. You got that? 17B ... Good. Okay, thank you. (*He hangs up the phone and then turns to* LILLY, *smiling proudly.*) Well, I've done it. I've called the police and they're on their way.

LILLY

Yes, you're right, Harold, now you've fucking done it, and you know what it's going to look like when they get here and find that there's no one here but you?

HAROLD

I know what you're thinking ... crazy, right? Well, you'll be here ... and then you'll look crazy too.

LILLY

Oh no I won't look crazy, because I won't be here.

HAROLD

You won't be here? What do you mean, you won't be here?

LILLY

I won't be here. Is that plain enough for you?

HAROLD

Wait a minute … where will you be?

LILLY

I'll be out on the fire escape.

HAROLD

On the *fire escape*?

LILLY

Yes. I don't want anyone seeing me in my nightgown, especially an irate police officer, who, I'm certain, will be very fucking upset when he finds out that he was called upon for absolutely no good reason at all. No, I'll just wait on the fire escape until he leaves. So there, you see … you will be the only moron here, and you will be the only one who looks crazy—not me.

HAROLD

Yeah, well, I won't look so crazy when they take that guy away in handcuffs, Lilly. You'll see.

LILLY

The only one they're going to take away is you, Harold, and it won't be in handcuffs; it will be in a straight jacket, like the time … remember when?

HAROLD

Oh, sure, you had to bring *that* up again, right? Just one time! Just one time that happened, Lilly, and you brand me for life. For Christ's sake, one time, a little mistake, and I get crucified for it over and over. Can't you ever forget that? Can't you ever forget that happened? It was a simple misunderstanding, that's all.

LILLY

A simple misunderstanding? You were running naked in Central Park! What's the misunderstanding?

HAROLD

Remember, there was a terrific heat wave that summer. I was only trying to cool off.

LILLY

It was December, Harold. Remember?

HAROLD

I don't think so, Lilly. I believe it was mid-July. Hot as hell.

LILLY

No, Harold, it was December. Don't you recall? You were singing "Deck the Halls with Harold's Balls" when the undercover policeman in the Santa costume tackled you and sat on your naked butt until the men in white coats arrived.

HAROLD

(With a face.) It was so long ago I'd nearly forgotten.

LILLY

How convenient.

HAROLD

I wish it would be as convenient for you. It's good to forget things once in a while, Lilly. You should try it. You may even like it.

LILLY

There are a great many things I'd like to forget, but they stay glued to my memory. I can't get rid of them no matter how hard I try.

HAROLD

Regardless of past events and what you may think of me, there is a man on our stove, and I saw him as plain as day, like I'm seeing you now.

LILLY

Exactly, so there you go.

HAROLD

What do you mean?

LILLY

Precisely, is what I mean. What do you mean?

HAROLD

I mean I'm here, you're here, he's here. We're all here …

LILLY

Are you certain? That's the question.

HAROLD

What's the question? I'm lost.

LILLY

It doesn't take much.

HAROLD

Is something in question, here?

LILLY

The question remains, am I here? Is he here? Are you here? Is anyone here? Can you be certain?

HAROLD

Lilly, you're confusing me. Isn't it enough that I saw someone on our stove? What are you asking?

LILLY

Am I asking, or is it you who is asking? That's the first question.

HAROLD

Well then, I'm asking if you're asking. You see, I can play this game too. You're not the only one who is going to be asking something around here! If you ask, then I'll ask. Then both of us will be asking. I just wish I knew *what* I was asking!

LILLY

I'm asking if you know what the truth is. I'm wondering if you understand the difference between reality and what it is that's in that little pea brain of yours. You think you're here, but maybe you're somewhere else and you only think you're here. That's possible, isn't it?

HAROLD

I suppose—I mean …

LILLY

Maybe you're still in the hospital, and you're dreaming that we're here. This could all very well be a nightmare, couldn't it?

HAROLD

Lilly, I don't think that—

LILLY

Or perhaps you're not in the hospital. Maybe you're only thirteen years old, and it's your secret desire to be with a woman. You could be a thirteen-year-old kid wanking off right now thinking about me and my doorbells.

HAROLD

I'd rather be twelve; thirteen is an unlucky number.

LILLY

Or wait! I know! Maybe it's the opposite—maybe you're really ninety years old, and this is something that happened to you sixty years ago, and you're *imagining* that it's happening now. A repressed image is what they call it. That's what this could be—a repressed image. Maybe that's it. Wouldn't that be the devil's joke?

HAROLD

No, if I'm going to be anything, I'm not going to be ninety. I'd much rather be twelve. *(Pauses.)* Lilly, one of us is not making sense.

LILLY

They say it's you.

HAROLD

I've heard that. *(Pauses.)* Who are they?

LILLY

They are those we've been talking to.

HAROLD

Come on, Lilly, how can they be those? They're two different words.

LILLY

They can be a lot of things. They can also be them.

HAROLD

I've never liked them or those. Come to think of it, I don't like *they* either. What do *they* want, anyway?

LILLY

They are looking for meaning.

HAROLD

They'll never find it. They'll never get more than a gist.

LILLY

They seem to be happy with that.

HAROLD

Well, I'm not happy with that, especially with what they pump into me. *They* are always giving me pills.

LILLY

They say you need them.

HAROLD

How do they know what I need?

LILLY

It seems that you're a type.

HAROLD

I'm more than a type; I'm a person. They don't know me. How can they know me? Do they come here for dinner to watch how I cook? Do they watch me do the wash? Clean the apartment? Iron my clothes? Does anyone really know another person? Is that possible? Do they know what I'm thinking? How I feel? What I want and where I want to end up? Of course they don't. They don't know a goddamn thing! They don't know me at all. And yet they think they know me, because I'm a type and not a person.

LILLY

Am I a person, Harold?

HAROLD

They say you're a type, too, Lilly.

LILLY

I don't like being a type, Harold.

HAROLD

You're my type, Lilly.

LILLY

Therein lies the problem.

HAROLD

I have no problem with that. You have no problem with
that. It's they, them, and those that have the problem,
and so they decide our life, our fate, and our destiny.
Well, I won't let them!

LILLY

I'm afraid there is nothing that you can do to prevent it.

HAROLD

Don't worry, Lilly. We'll outsmart 'em. I still have a trick
up my sleeve.

LILLY

I don't know, Harold; they seem to have the upper
hand.

HAROLD

Momentarily, is all.

LILLY

Our last stand didn't go well, did it?

HAROLD

That's because they had the home-court advantage.

LILLY

You shouldn't have run amok.

HAROLD

I couldn't help myself. They wouldn't let me get a word in edgewise. They ignored me as if I wasn't there. I was a piece of paper on the table, a magazine in a rack, a stain in the carpet. They kept talking among themselves, and at us—not to us. I kept raising my hand like they told me. Remember, they said, "Don't shout out. Never shout out. If you feel you need to say something, raise your hand." So I raised my hand. They never looked at me. I raised my hand and waved it. I raised my hand and waved it. I raised and waved my hand so much I felt like a flag fucking. *(He pauses, angry that he reversed the words.* LILLY *shakes her head and eyes the ceiling.)* Anyway, I almost waved my hand right off my arm. They never saw it, or if they did, they pretended not to notice.

LILLY

We were outnumbered.

HAROLD

Oh, I'm glad you noticed that. They do that, you know. They do that on purpose. If there are two of us, there are three of them. If we went in with four, they'd have five. It makes them feel superior.

LILLY

It gives them the upper edge.

HAROLD

And they stick together. Did you notice that too?

LILLY

Like glue.

HAROLD

Not one of them ever questions the other. There were three of them in that room, but there was only one voice.

LILLY

Not everyone spoke.

HAROLD

Ah, brilliant observation! Did you see that woman—the skinny one with the beady eyes? She kept looking over her glasses at us like we were fish in a market place. *(He puts his head on his chest, pretending to look over glasses.)* She never uttered a word, that one.

LILLY

She took notes.

HAROLD

I saw that! She took notes. She was the only one taking notes. I wish I could have seen what was in those notes. *(Pause.)* I should have taken notes.

LILLY

Oh, yeah, a lot of fucking good that would have done us. I can see you now, writing: *(Pretends she's writing on a clipboard.)* And then I ran amok! Yes, we'd want a record of that, for sure.

HAROLD

I had to do something, I tell you. They wouldn't let me speak! It was as if they put a sock in my mouth.

LILLY

I'm afraid, Harold. I'm afraid of what is going to happen to us.

HAROLD

Don't worry, Lilly; I still have a trick up my sleeve.

LILLY

I'd rather not hear about your trick, okay, Harold?

HAROLD

They'll never expect it.

LILLY

I don't want to hear about it. I'm too frightened. I need to go to sleep. Tell me I'm bored, Harold.

HAROLD

You're bored, Lilly.

LILLY

You know something, Harold? This conversation is beginning to bore me. I'm going to sleep.

(LILLY *lies down, turns over and pulls the covers up around her neck.* HAROLD *is in a heightened state of nervousness, biting his nails, placing his ear against the door, and pacing to and fro. After some moments,* LILLY *picks her head up.)*

LILLY

Harold, what the hell are you doing? Quit it, will you? Stop pacing.

HAROLD

I'm too nervous to sit still. Why is he crying?

LILLY

Why is who crying, Harold?

HAROLD

(Pointing at the door.) Him! That … that guy out there—
that man on our stove! He's crying—well, he's not really
crying—it's more like he's … sniffling.

LILLY

Sniffling? Did you say he was sniffling?

HAROLD

Yes. He's sniffling, not crying. He's definitely sniffling.
(Puts his ear against the door.) He's on our stove, right
now, this minute, sniffling. I think I hear him.

LILLY

Oh, that explains it. Why didn't you tell me that before?
He's a stove sniffler, Harold. Don't you know? There's a
lot of that going around New York City lately. In fact,
Mrs. Higgins, down the hall, was telling me just the
other day that she had a stove sniffler in her apartment
the other night—couldn't get rid of him. He sniffled all
night long. Kept her up until four in the morning. A
stove sniffler—you *are* a freakin' loon! I'm outta here.
(She lies down and pulls the covers over her head.)

HAROLD

What's he doing here—that guy? What does he want?
He's giving me the creeps, Lilly. He's making me very
nervous. He's making me think of bad dreams. I think
he was a bad dream I had one night, and … and now

he's here. I have bad dreams all the time. Do you know that? They pop into my head when I least expect it. They follow me and haunt me. They suffocate me. They keep coming back time and time again. Why do they come back, Lilly? Why do they come back to haunt me?

LILLY

(From under the covers.) I don't know, Harold; maybe it's something you ate.

HAROLD

No, Lilly, it's not anything I ate. These dreams come back whether I've eaten or not. And when they do, I think of you.

LILLY

Me? You think of me? What do you think of?

HAROLD

I think of your doorbells. Thinking of your doorbells helps me to get the bad dreams out of my head.

LILLY

I'm happy they serve a purpose.

HAROLD

(Puts his hand on his head.) Oh my God! I just thought of something terrible. What if he should have only three fingers on one hand?

LILLY

(Lifts her head out from under the covers.) I'm sorry, would you mind repeating that?

HAROLD

What?

LILLY

The thing you just said ... you know, the last thing ... the terrible thing ... the part about the fingers.

HAROLD

I said, "What if he should have only three fingers on one hand?"

LILLY

Hmmm ... that's what I thought you said. And why might that be a big problem, Harold?

HAROLD

Because ...

LILLY

Yes, go on.

HAROLD

Because that's one of my worst dreams. It's something that happened to me when I was a child, and it still haunts me. I'm terrified of people who are missing two fingers.

LILLY

How is it I don't know this about you, Harold? Why have you never told me this?

HAROLD

We've never been in this situation before.

LILLY

I think we have.

HAROLD

No, Lilly, we've been in a lot of situations, but we've never been in *this* situation before. I would have remembered.

LILLY

I suppose there are some consolations in life. *(Pauses for a while. They look at each other. He's waiting for her to say something.)* I'm hesitating here; can you feel it?

HAROLD

You rarely hesitate, Lilly. This must be serious.

LILLY

I'm hesitating because I know I'm going to regret asking the next question, but it seems you leave me no choice. So tell me, Harold, why are you so terrified of people who are missing two fingers?

HAROLD

When I was a kid, the man next door lost two fingers in an accident with an electric saw he kept in his basement. *(Squirming.)* He said that when his fingers got cut off, they flopped around on his table like two little fish out of water. *(Wincing.)* He said he picked them up and put them in a jar filled with water. He told me that whenever he puts the light on in his basement, those two fingers squirm around in that jar. He called them his unlucky dancing fingers. He used to tell me this story all the time, and then he'd stick that deformed hand in my face and say, "Wanna shake on it?" Ugh … I still dream about that ugly hand and those unlucky dancing fingers squirming around in that jar. It makes me shiver just thinking about them.

LILLY

You are a loon. A fucking loon.

HAROLD

Oh my God, Lilly—I just thought of something else! When the police get here, I won't be able to answer the door!

LILLY

I'm almost afraid to ask why.

HAROLD

If I answer the door, I'll have to go right past that man on our stove.

LILLY

That's right.

HAROLD

What if he has a gun?

LILLY

You should have thought of that *before* you called the police. *(The doorbell rings. She grabs her breasts.)* Ah, speaking of doorbells …

(HAROLD *reaches for the bedroom doorknob and pauses.)*

Well, what are you waiting for? Aren't you going to answer the door?

(The doorbell rings again. HAROLD *pauses, looking back and forth between* LILLY *and the door. Now there is a loud bang on the door.)*

THE POLICEMAN

(Offstage.) Mr. Jerkins, open up! It's the police. Mr. Jerkins?

LILLY

I'd do something about now, if I were you.

THE POLICEMAN

(Offstage, banging on the door.) Mr. Jerkins? Are you in there?

HAROLD

Yes, I'm coming! *(To* LILLY.*)* Oh my God, Lilly, I'm so nervous. Help me through this, will you?

LILLY

What do you want me to do?

HAROLD

I don't know; think of something.

LILLY

Why don't you wank off?

HAROLD

Good idea. (HAROLD *jumps into bed and lies down.)*

LILLY

I was kidding! You can't do that now! You've got a fucking cop at the door! Get out of this bed! *(She points toward the door.)* Get out there, *now!*

HAROLD

(Scrambling out of bed.) Yes, yes, I'm going. I'm going now to answer the door, all right? It seems I have no choice.

LILLY

Hurry up and get out there! One thing though, before you go.

HAROLD

Yes, yes? What is it? Will you miss me if something bad happens to me? Is that it?

LILLY

Is your life insurance up to date?

HAROLD

Very funny, Lilly. You're so kind. I don't know how to thank you for your kindness.

LILLY

Think nothing of it, fucker.

HAROLD

Okay, I'm going out there now. The way I see it, there's only one way to do this without getting killed. I'll dodge and weave my way to the door. All the while, I'll be screaming. The screaming will distract the guy on the stove, and if he tries to shoot me, maybe he'll miss, because I'll be dodging and weaving. Sound good?

LILLY

Sounds like a very good plan. But if I were you, I'd be careful; with all that screaming and dodging, I wouldn't be surprised if the policeman shoots you.

(HAROLD *looks at* LILLY, *surprised that it might actually happen. He then realizes she's pulling his leg. He smiles sarcastically and unlocks the door. He takes a deep breath, turns off the lamp, opens the bedroom door, flicks on the living room light, shuts the bedroom door, and then begins screaming, contorting his body, and dodging and weaving his way toward the door. When he arrives, he stops screaming, flicks a light switch, and opens the door.* THE POLICEMAN *rushes in, his hand on his gun. The strange man is no longer on the stove.)*

THE POLICEMAN
What's going on? You have an intruder?

HAROLD
Oh yes, officer; thank you so much for coming. Someone is here—a strange man. I had just gone to sleep when I heard these weird noises coming from the kitchen. I got out of bed, came out here, flicked on the kitchen light, and there he was, on the stove. (HAROLD *points toward the now vacant stove.)*

THE POLICEMAN
On the stove, you say? Do you know the guy?

HAROLD
No, officer. I never saw him before in my life.

THE POLICEMAN
Did you get a good look at him?

HAROLD

Yes … a fairly good look.

THE POLICEMAN

Well, what's he look like?

HAROLD

Very strange.

THE POLICEMAN

Strange? How?

HAROLD

Well … he was extremely thin, and he was wearing very tight clothes. He wore a black-and-white striped shirt and black pants. What else … oh yes, he had a black stocking cap on his head. It didn't cover his face; it just sort of sat on his head. But you know, the strangest thing about him was his skin. It was white—pure white.

THE POLICEMAN

(*Stroking his chin.*) What was he doing?

HAROLD

Nothing. He was just crouching on the stove, sniffling.

THE POLICEMAN

Sniffling?

HAROLD

Yes. Some people might call it crying, but a more appropriate description would be sniffling. Yes, he was definitely sniffling.

THE POLICEMAN

Okay, so let me get this straight. This guy was just sitting on your stove, sniffling. He wasn't doing anything else.

HAROLD

Well, to be quite frank, he wasn't actually sitting. He was *crouching* on top of the stove.

THE POLICEMAN

Crouching?

HAROLD

Yeah, you know—crouching. (*To illustrate,* HAROLD *assumes an awkward, semicrouching position, almost falling over.*)

THE POLICEMAN

(*Stroking his chin.*) Hmmm. What was that screaming I heard before you opened the door?

HAROLD

Oh, that was Lilly. She was afraid I might get shot when I ran past the stranger to let you in.

THE POLICEMAN

There's someone here with you?

HAROLD

Yes, Lilly is with me. She's in the bedroom … I think.

THE POLICEMAN

All right, enough of this. Let's search the apartment.

(THE POLICEMAN *searches the apartment. He looks under furniture, opens the bathroom door and looks in.* HAROLD *stands, watching from the living room.* THE POLICEMAN *walks into the bedroom and turns on the lamp.* LILLY *is not there. The bed is made up where she had been sleeping.* THE POLICEMAN *searches the bedroom, looking under the bed. He turns off the bedroom lamp, shutting the door, and re-enters the living room.*)

THE POLICEMAN

I thought you said that someone was here with you?

HAROLD

Yes … Lilly.

THE POLICEMAN

Okay, so where is she?

HAROLD

Who?

THE POLICEMAN

The woman who is supposed to be in the bedroom?

HAROLD

Oh, you mean Lilly. Have you met her? Isn't she lovely?

THE POLICEMAN

No, I haven't met her; that's what I'm trying to explain. Where the hell is she?

HAROLD

She said she didn't want you to see her in her nightgown, so she was going to wait on the fire escape until after you've left.

THE POLICEMAN

The fire escape? What fire escape? All right, I get the picture now. That's enough of this. Okay, Mr. Jerkins—

HAROLD

It's Jenkins.

THE POLICEMAN

Mr. Jenkins ... I searched all the rooms, and there's no sign of anyone. Your door was locked when you let me in, so this guy couldn't have gone out that way, period! You were in the bedroom, so I don't think—

HAROLD

Oh! So what are you saying, officer? Do you think I imagined all this? Do you think no one was here? I bet you think I didn't see anyone. Am I right? You think I'm crazy fucking! *(Pauses, shaking his fist, angry he's reversed the curse word again.)* Well, I'm not crazy! I know what I saw, and I saw someone!

THE POLICEMAN

I didn't say you were crazy, Mr. Jerkins—

HAROLD

JENKINS!

THE POLICEMAN

Oh, yeah, right—sorry—Mr. Jenkins. Look, maybe you're a little confused, that's all. You were sleeping, and then you heard a noise. You got up, it was dark, you thought you saw someone …

HAROLD

I did see someone! How many times must I say that?

THE POLICEMAN

Look, I ain't saying you did; I ain't saying you didn't … All I'm saying is this whole thing is going to look a whole lot better in the a.m. So, why not retire for the evening, get some shut-eye, and tomorrow morning, if you want to come down to the station and fill out a report, I'm certain the officer in charge will help you. Here's the address. *(He writes on a slip of paper and hands it to* HAROLD.*)* Like I said, you come down to the station tomorrow and the desk sergeant will be happy to assist you. How's about that?

HAROLD

Yes, okay. I'll come down in the morning and fill out a report. Because I did see someone, and I need to fill out a report! You never know who else is going to see this guy, and then they'll have to fill out a report, too. Then you'll have two reports! Maybe even three. I got word just today that there's been other sightings of stove snifflers in the neighborhood. I'm certain with a prolonged investigation you'll find stove snifflers throughout the city.

THE POLICEMAN

Yeah, okay. Whatever. (THE POLICEMAN *walks toward the door.)*

HAROLD

Ah ... excuse me, officer ... before you go ...

THE POLICEMAN

Yes, what is it?

HAROLD

(Points to the chair in the dining room. Leans in close to THE POLICEMAN.*)* Do you see anyone sitting in that chair?

THE POLICEMAN

(Looks with suspicion at the chair and then back at HAROLD.*)* No, of course not.

HAROLD

Are you sure?

THE POLICEMAN

Yeah, I'm certain of it.

HAROLD

That's good. *(Points with his thumb over his shoulder back toward the kitchen.)* What about on the stove? Do you see anyone on the stove?

THE POLICEMAN

(Looks over at the stove. Shakes his head.) Not a soul.

HAROLD

(Nodding.) That's a good sign … for both of us.

THE POLICEMAN

Yeah … okay … whatever. Get some rest tonight, Mr. Jerkins, and we'll see you in the morning. (THE POLICEMAN *exits.)*

HAROLD

(Yelling into the hall.) That's Jenkins! JENKINS! Do you hear me? It's JENKINS! *(Comes back into the apartment, shutting the door.)* What an idiot fucking!

(HAROLD *locks the door and turns off the lights in the dining room and living room. The stage is black. He enters the bedroom, closes the door and turns on his lamp.* LILLY *is back in bed, sitting up.)*

LILLY

I told you, didn't I?

(HAROLD *winces, takes off his robe, hangs it on the back of the door, removes his slippers and climbs into bed.)*

LILLY

You are fucking stupid, do you know that? I told you there was no one here. You know I'm always right, so why didn't you believe me? But no, you had to be right. You had to prove me wrong. You had to call the police. Don't you know the police can cause us trouble? They can put you back anytime they want … and there's nothing you can do about it. How would you like that, Mr. Smarty Pants? Then where would we be? Tell me, Harold, then where would we be? Right back to square one. Damn! *Stupid! Stupid! Stupid! Harold is stupid!*

(HAROLD turns away from LILLY and turns out the light. The stage is dark.)

LILLY

(After a moment.) AND DON'T YOU EVEN DARE *DREAM* ABOUT DOORBELLS!

End of Act One

Act Two

(The next night, just before midnight. Lights are on in the kitchen and the living room. The bedroom is dark. The dining table is clean. HAROLD, *dressed in his pajamas, robe and slippers, is bolting the front door. He checks that it is locked three times. He then searches the apartment, looking in the bathroom and under and behind furniture. Satisfied that the strange man is not in the apartment, he shuts all the lights and walks into the darkened bedroom. He closes the door and turns on his nightstand lamp.* LILLY, *dressed in a white cotton nightgown, is sitting up in bed, doing nothing.)*

LILLY

Are you satisfied that there is no one in the apartment?

HAROLD

(*Removes his robe, hangs it on the back of the door. He then removes his slippers and gets into bed.*) We're good.

LILLY

Are you certain? Perhaps you want some towels?

HAROLD

Towels? For what?

LILLY

To stuff under the doors. We wouldn't want anyone creeping in through the cracks, would we?

HAROLD

I was thinking I might invest in a motion detector.

LILLY

Now there's an idea.

HAROLD

A good one, don't you think?

LILLY

One of your best.

HAROLD

I thought I'd install it in the dining room. That way it would sweep the entire apartment.

LILLY

Whatever you do, don't install it near your brain; it will never go off.

HAROLD

If I install it near your mouth, it will never stop ringing.

LILLY

You'd kill the poor thing if you put it down the front of your pants.

HAROLD

Ah, but what a way to go.

LILLY

While in the saddle.

HAROLD

While in the pink.

LILLY

Out with a bang.

HAROLD

Dying for sex.

LILLY

Who? You or the machine?

HAROLD

Both of us, I suppose.

LILLY

Let's not get a motion detector.

HAROLD

Do I detect a hint of jealousy?

LILLY

Harold, if I want to tell you something, you'll be given a lot more than a fucking hint.

HAROLD

You needn't worry, Lilly; I'm yours—all of me.

LILLY

And I'm all you, Harold.

HAROLD

Lilly, I'm afraid that sniffling guy is going to show up again tonight.

LILLY

I wouldn't worry about that.

HAROLD

No? Why?

LILLY

Stove snifflers rarely show up two nights in a row.

HAROLD

That's a relief.

LILLY

Your troubles are hardly over, however.

HAROLD

What do you mean?

LILLY

I hear that a sink sitter usually follows a stove sniffler.

HAROLD

A sink sitter? What's that?

LILLY

That's someone you'll find late at night sitting in your sink. They don't sniffle. They sing "Row, Row, Row Your Boat Gently Down the Drain" all night long. It drives people crazy. But there's no risk of that happening to you; you're already there.

HAROLD

You had me worried for a second.

LILLY

You have me worried all the time. Now promise me that you'll stay in bed tonight no matter what you hear. Whatever sound you think you hear is only your imagination playing tricks on you. Remember, nothing is real.

HAROLD

That's what they tell me.

LILLY

You can believe them. They know.

HAROLD

But *how* do they know, Lilly? What makes them so certain?

LILLY

They are the powers that be, Harold.

HAROLD

Are they ever wrong?

LILLY

Lots of times.

HAROLD

Well, maybe they're wrong now.

LILLY

I hope so. I don't like the idea of us being separated.

HAROLD

I don't like it either. We need to do something.

LILLY

What did you have in mind?

HAROLD

I was about to ask you.

LILLY

I'm stumped.

HAROLD

I'm clueless.

LILLY

You'd think it would be obvious.

HAROLD

Apparent.

LILLY

Evident.

HAROLD

Understandable.

LILLY

Harold, I'm frightened.

HAROLD

The game's not up yet; I still have one trick up my sleeve.

LILLY

And what might that be?

HAROLD

It's extreme, but …

LILLY

Yes, but will it work?

HAROLD

Definitely … I just wish I could think of an alternative. *(Pauses.)* Wait; I know. Why don't we switch places?

LILLY

Who? You and I? That would be awkward, wouldn't it?

HAROLD

No, I wasn't talking about you and me. I was referring to us and the powers that be.

LILLY

That would be more awkward.

HAROLD

Why? We can do it. I'm certain of it. *(Pauses, thinking.)* How does one become the powers that be?

LILLY

You study hard, you work hard, you kiss a lot of ass.

HAROLD

Oh. I don't think I'd be very good at that.

LILLY

What? Ass kissing?

HAROLD

No, the study and work hard part. It's beyond me. I'd be terrific at ass kissing, though. I can see myself now, working for a pretty little boss, kissing her ass all day long. I'd enjoy that.

LILLY

Suppose your boss were a man?

HAROLD

A man, eh?

LILLY

Yep, you could be working for a man, you know.

HAROLD

Hmmm, a man, eh?

LILLY

Yes, a man. You've heard of them, haven't you?

HAROLD

Gee, I never thought of that.

LILLY

Here's your chance.

HAROLD

Interesting concept.

LILLY

It's attention grabbing, that's for sure. Would you be willing to let yourself go with a man?

HAROLD

I never imagined …

LILLY

Don't let me stand in your way.

HAROLD

I could see where it might open up new and exciting possibilities.

LILLY

Endless.

HAROLD

Boundless.

LILLY

Limitless.

HAROLD

Massive.

LILLY

That would be one way to describe it.

HAROLD

Enormous.

LILLY

That too.

HAROLD

Deep.

LILLY

Let's not go there.

HAROLD

Dark.

LILLY

I'll say.

HAROLD

Cavernous.

LILLY

A bottomless pit.

HAROLD

Are you certain we're talking about the same thing?

LILLY

It depends upon which way you're going.

HAROLD

Which way should I be going?

LILLY

Bottoms up.

HAROLD

Lilly, why do I get the feeling that you're always one step ahead of me?

LILLY

A feeling, is it?

HAROLD

Yes, like you're walking much too fast.

LILLY

Funny, I get the same feeling in reverse.

HAROLD

It seems you always have an advantage.

LILLY

I believe it has something to do with intelligence.

HAROLD

What are you saying, that you're smarter than I am?

LILLY

Fucking light-years away.

HAROLD

I don't believe that. There has to be another reason.

LILLY

Oh, no—not another fucking meaning of life discussion.

HAROLD

It must have something to do with positioning.

LILLY

Positioning?

HAROLD

Yes, everything has to do with positioning—your position in work, your position in the family, your position in life. We are responsible for the position we create. *(He looks down at her butt.)* And I notice—you're positioned far more forward than I am.

LILLY

(Looking down at her butt.) That's the reason I'm smarter?

HAROLD

More than likely. Positioning.

LILLY

What will you have me do?

HAROLD

Move back.

LILLY

(She slides her butt back.) There. Any better?

HAROLD

(Pauses.) Give it time to work.

LILLY

I don't know about you, but I feel fucking dumber already, just by trying this.

HAROLD

(He brings his palm to the top of her head without touching her and then moves it to the top of his head.) You're taller than I am.

LILLY

I never noticed that.

HAROLD

That could make all the difference in the world.

LILLY

What shall I do?

HAROLD

Slouch down a bit.

LILLY

(She slouches down a bit.) Like this?

HAROLD

(He measures again and finds they're the same height.) More.

LILLY

(She slouches more.) How's this?

HAROLD

(Measuring again, he finds he's taller.) Perfect.

LILLY

Do you feel any difference yet?

HAROLD

I'm beginning to.

LILLY

Do you feel smarter?

HAROLD

I think I am.

LILLY

I feel like a fucking jackass. But that's okay, because now I can ask you the dumb questions that you ask me.

HAROLD

I didn't say that.

LILLY

Hey, look, you're the smart one around here now, which means you're the one to go to. Right?

HAROLD

I suppose, but …

LILLY

The smart ones are the ones in charge. They're the ones who know better. They have all the answers. They keep the ship from sinking. Isn't that right?

HAROLD

Is that true?

LILLY

Absolutely. You are now the captain of the ship. You're in charge. Bring her round, Captain!

HAROLD

Hey, wait a minute; I didn't know I'd have to steer a ship.

LILLY

Man the sails!

HAROLD

What?

LILLY

Heave to, and all that other stuff!

HAROLD

Do I have to know these things?

LILLY

Of course you do. You have to plot a course, too.

HAROLD

I don't know how to plot a course.

LILLY

Well, you'd better learn. You have to plot a course, steer the ship, and take the heat.

HAROLD

Take the heat?

LILLY

Absolutely! You're in charge, so you have to take the heat if there are any mishaps, even those you can't control.

HAROLD

I had no idea.

LILLY

You haven't heard the best part yet.

HAROLD

There's more?

LILLY

There's always more. When the seas are rough and the boat doesn't look like it's going to make it, the captain *always* goes down with the ship.

HAROLD

Goes down with the ship? Hold on, I had no idea—

LILLY

So tell me, Captain, what is the best strategy for staying out of the fucking mental ward? And how many times can we do it so that we don't go over the limit? And how do we get to stay together and tell Dr. Carney to go fuck himself?

(HAROLD *looks down at his butt, compares its position to* LILLY's *and moves backward. He crouches down and measures. He thinks he might now be on par with her head. He crouches down further. He exhales deeply, smiles at her, lies down, pulls the covers up, and turns out the lamp. The stage is dark. After a minute or so, we hear sniffling.* HAROLD *turns on his lamp. He listens without disturbing* LILLY, *who is sleeping. He creeps out of bed, puts on his robe and slippers, and turns out the lamp. He opens the bedroom door, walks out of the room, closes the door, flicks on the living room lava lamp, and tip-toes into the dining area, slinking toward the kitchen. He turns on the kitchen light. However, this time, the stranger is hiding behind the dining room table. As* HAROLD *makes* his way into the kitchen, the stranger sneaks up behind him and taps him on the shoulder. HAROLD screams and falls on the floor. He trembles as the stranger approaches. HAROLD tries to get away, but he backs into a wall. The stranger stands over him. The stranger is dressed as he was the night before.)

FRUSTRATO

(Sniffling.) I don't want to be here! I don't want to be here!

HAROLD

(Pauses, waiting for something to happen.) Well?

FRUSTRATO

Well, what?

HAROLD

Well, are you just going to stand there?

FRUSTRATO

What would you have me do?

HAROLD

I don't know, but shouldn't you be doing *something*?

FRUSTRATO

I'm certain I will once I think of something appropriate.

HAROLD

Let me see your hands. How many fingers do you have?

(FRUSTRATO *raises clenched fists. One-by-one, he slowly stretches out his fingers.* HAROLD *counts to ten. Satisfied, he slowly stands up.*)

FRUSTRATO

Were you expecting less than ten?

HAROLD

What are you doing here? What do you want?

FRUSTRATO

I was summoned.

HAROLD

What are you talking about? Who summoned you?

FRUSTRATO

You did!

HAROLD

Me? Why, I did nothing of the sort. Who are you?

FRUSTRATO

My name is Frustrato.

HAROLD

You're a foreigner.

FRUSTRATO

Do I look like someone who comes from your neighborhood?

HAROLD

You don't look like anyone I know.

FRUSTRATO

I'd know you anywhere, even if you were disguised. I sometimes have trouble recognizing myself, however. Do you think I look older?

HAROLD

How would I know; I didn't know you before.

FRUSTRATO

Before what?

HAROLD

Before tonight.

FRUSTRATO

On the contrary, you know me very well. Look closely.

(HAROLD *stares closely into* FRUSTRATO's *eyes.* FRUSTRATO *stares back.* HAROLD, *staring, slowly moves to the right;*

FRUSTRATO *moves with him. The pair move in unison to the left, then up, then down. Then right and left again.)*

HAROLD

Nope. I can't say I know you.

FRUSTRATO

Oh, you know me, all right. You just don't recognize me now that I'm … mature.

HAROLD

What are you doing here?

FRUSTRATO

I'm the replacement.

HAROLD

The replacement? For what?

FRUSTRATO

For Lilly.

HAROLD

For Lilly?

FRUSTRATO

(Looks around the ceiling) Is there an echo in here? Yes, I'm the replacement. You do know what a replacement is.

HAROLD

Yes, it's a noun indicating one thing filling in for another.

FRUSTRATO

Correct! A substitute.

HAROLD

An alternate?

FRUSTRATO

An exchange.

HAROLD

A switch?

FRUSTRATO

A swap.

HAROLD

Someone to take the place of.

FRUSTRATO

Someone instead of.

HAROLD

An understudy?

FRUSTRATO

(Pauses. He looks at the audience, then back at Harold with a look of consternation.) Not on your life.

HAROLD

I'm a bit confused. Tell me again, who are you replacing?

FRUSTRATO

Lilly.

HAROLD

Lilly? You don't mean …

FRUSTRATO

Yes, I mean it, and I'll be mean about it if it doesn't happen very soon.

HAROLD

Forget it! I won't stand for it.

FRUSTRATO

You have no choice.

HAROLD

There's always a choice.

FRUSTRATO

You heard Dr. Carney. He's ordered you to get rid of her. She's not working out. Sorry, she has to go, and that's final.

HAROLD

I thought we had more time.

FRUSTRATO

Rubbish! You were at the office today to plead your case. It didn't go well, did it?

HAROLD

How do you know all this?

FRUSTRATO

It's the replacement's job to know these things.

HAROLD

Well, you've come too soon. I need more time.

FRUSTRATO

It's always a matter of time, isn't it? Time, time, time. It always boils down to time. No time for this, no time for that. If only I had more time. Time, time, time. I'd do it if I had the time. Can't stop; I have no time. Time and time again. A stitch in time. Time is on our side. Time will tell. Time in. Time out. Time, time, time. Well, Harold, guess what? Your time has run out. The clock has struck twelve; Lilly is turning back into a pumpkin; and you, my friend, are, like the cheese, standing alone, and it's *time* you realize that.

HAROLD

This is happening much too fast.

FRUSTRATO

Fast is how it should happen. Don't slowly pull the bandage from your boo-boo. Pull the sucker off fast as lightning. It hurts less that way. Besides, you'll have so much more fun with me. I'll be kinder, gentler. I'll be like a bird, a dove, a *white* dove. I'll flutter, I'll coo. Coo. Coo. Coo. My feathers will never get ruffled. I shan't call you stupid, and I won't make you angry.

HAROLD

Shhh, listen. What do you hear?

FRUSTRATO

(Listening.) Horses?

HAROLD

No.

FRUSTRATO

Waves crashing against the beach? Is that it?

HAROLD

No!

FRUSTRATO

Wait, I know! Popcorn, popping? Yes. Right? Am I close?

HAROLD

No!

FRUSTRATO

Oh please, give me another shot at it. I'm certain I'll do better next time. Okay, never mind. I give up.

HAROLD

I thought I heard Lilly. I guess not. But just to be certain … (HAROLD *tiptoes to the bedroom and puts his ear against the door. He then tiptoes back to* FRUSTRATO.) Please keep your voice down. Lilly is asleep, and she would be very angry if she knew I was talking to you.

FRUSTRATO

She gets angry a lot, doesn't she?

(HAROLD *pauses, then looks back toward the bedroom door. He walks over to the dining room table and sits.* FRUSTRATO *stands over him.*)

HAROLD

Lilly has a tendency to get angry, but—

FRUSTRATO

(Almost hissing.) I know. I can help you. Let *me* be your friend.

HAROLD

Lilly is my friend. She's been with me for so long. It's always been Lilly. We belong together. We're like two peas in a pod.

FRUSTRATO

No you're not. You're total opposites. You're yin and yang.

HAROLD

We're pencil and paper.

FRUSTRATO

You're night and day.

HAROLD

We're shoes and socks.

FRUSTRATO

You're black and white.

HAROLD

We're Robin and Marion, Fred and Ginger, Abbott and Costello, and I will not be separated from Lilly! Besides, I need her. She helps me.

FRUSTRATO

That's not what I hear.

HAROLD

Then you must have a hearing problem. Oh, I get it. It's them again, isn't it? *Them* sent you, didn't they? Or *they* did. Or was it *those*? The little one with the beady eyes who never says anything—I bet she put you up to this. Am I right?

FRUSTRATO

You're not list-en-ing. It was *you* who sent for me. Look, there comes a time in every man's life when he must separate himself from those he's been around a long time so that he can grow as a person. You're not growing. It's only natural that you want someone to help you get through the separation. Hence me.

HAROLD

I stopped growing years ago.

FRUSTRATO

Precisely.

HAROLD

Why would I want to grow any more than I already have? I'm happy being my size. Besides, I won't fit into my clothes if I grow any more.

FRUSTRATO

You're missing the point.

HAROLD

I didn't know there was a point.

FRUSTRATO

There's always a point, and you've reached a point in your life where you need a change.

HAROLD

A change of what?

FRUSTRATO

A change of everything. Look, every species on the planet has children. Kids grow up, and they leave the nest to live their own lives. They grow into mature adults—well, not all humans, but that's another subject that we'll touch on at a later date. Don't you see? Now it's your turn to grow up. Leave the nest. Spread your wings! Soar like an eagle!

HAROLD

Why can't I spread my wings with Lilly?

FRUSTRATO

Because she's the one holding you down! She's the one stopping you from growing up.

HAROLD

She helps me.

FRUSTRATO

How does she help you?

HAROLD

She gives me discipline. And Dr. Carney said I need discipline.

FRUSTRATO

Discipline, shmiscipline! She gives you a headache, that's what she gives you. She stops you from doing the things you want—the things you like to do. Without her, you can do whatever you want—any time you want. We can have fun together, you and I. We can do anything you want. *Anything!*

HAROLD

Anything? Even … you know what?

FRUSTRATO

(Hissing.) Yesss … Anything … Even … you know what.

HAROLD

That opens up possibilities, doesn't it?

FRUSTRATO

(He jumps on the back of HAROLD's *chair. Bending over, he speaks into* HAROLD's *ear.)* Limitless possibilities ... and combinations. Remember how Lilly used to make you feel good? *(He moves his hands up and down, tapping his fingers against* HAROLD's *body.)*

HAROLD

Like she was painting a picture, every stroke a masterpiece.

FRUSTRATO

(Jumping off the chair.) Lilly doesn't do that anymore, does she? She's dropped the brushes, thrown down her pallet, rolled up the canvas.

HAROLD

Yes, she stopped painting a long time ago. *(Pauses.)* But we're not supposed to do that anymore. Dr. Carney says I have to have discipline. Without discipline I'll be locked up, and I *never* want to go back there!

FRUSTRATO

Discipline, shmiscipline! Who's going to find out? If Lilly's not here, no one will ever know. She's the one who rats you out, you know. Get rid of her, and you can do whatever you want! You can have whatever you want. It's all in the palm of your hand. You have the power.

HAROLD

I have power?

FRUSTRATO

More than you know. You've been hiding behind this mask of ignorance and foolishness for so long you don't remember who you really are and what you are capable of. You've reinvented yourself, Harold, and I must say, it's been on the cheap. "Why is that?" I ask myself. You used to be brilliant, fearless, confident. Now look at you. A nothing.

HAROLD

I used to be a something.

FRUSTRATO

You were a great something.

HAROLD

Now I am a nothing.

FRUSTRATO

A zero.

HAROLD

A nil.

FRUSTRATO

A naught.

HAROLD

A zilch.

FRUSTRATO

A nobody.

HAROLD

A has-been.

FRUSTRATO

A wash-up.

HAROLD

Yesterday's news.

FRUSTRATO

A total waste.

HAROLD

An inferior.

FRUSTRATO

A loser.

HAROLD

(Pauses.) I've lost track; who are we talking about?

FRUSTRATO

You, Harold. You were once a great man, remember? Smart, you were. What did you graduate with? A three point eight?

HAROLD

Three point nine.

FRUSTRATO

After college, you had the world by the balls. They all wanted you, didn't they? And you went with the best, because you *were* the best. Money came easy to you. You were respected.

HAROLD

Admired.

FRUSTRATO

Popular.

HAROLD

Well liked.

FRUSTRATO

Loved.

HAROLD

Recognized.

FRUSTRATO

Envied.

HAROLD

Are we still talking about me?

FRUSTRATO

Yes.

HAROLD

Admired.

FRUSTRATO

But Lilly was there. She was always there, hiding in the background, waiting for the right moment to pounce and turn you upside down.

HAROLD

(Smiling.) Ah, the good old days.

FRUSTRATO

She did it slowly. First, there were the little conversations between the two of you. In the beginning, no one paid attention. But then, as the conversations grew, people began to wonder.

HAROLD

Speculate.

FRUSTRATO

Doubt.

HAROLD

I began to doubt.

FRUSTRATO

Then, one day, she appeared in all her glory, making you crazy with her incessant talking. She was persistent— persistent! She has a power over you, and you give in to her every time. *Stop! Right here, right now!* Stop listening to her. She's a repression, an oppression, a subjugation, an insignificance, an albatross around your neck, and a blotch upon your character, your personality, and your life. That's why they watch you.

HAROLD

(Looking to and fro.) They do? They watch me? Oh, I knew it.

FRUSTRATO

Listening to Lilly puts you on the hard road. If you continue, you'll wind up in the same ditch you once fell into and couldn't climb out of. Get rid of her, Harold. You can do it. I can help.

HAROLD

(Laying his head upon the table.) I can't! I've tried! I've tried! So many times I've tried. You don't understand …

FRUSTRATO

Oh, I understand, all right. That's why I'm here. I'm here to help you rid yourself of her. I can do it. *We* can do it. You'll see. *(Pauses.)* We've met before, you know.

HAROLD

(Picks up his head.) We have?

FRUSTRATO

Yes, it was a while ago. I didn't look like this. I was a dog.

HAROLD

A dog?

FRUSTRATO

Not just any dog, Harold. I was your dog—your little puppy dog in the ward. I used to visit you in the evening when no one was looking. Remember? It was when they took Lilly away from you.

HAROLD

Yes! They took her away from me. She screamed, you know. Oh, she screamed something terrible. Did you hear her screaming when they took her? Every night she screamed. "Let me in! Let me in!" The screams were awful. She wouldn't let me sleep. Every time I closed my eyes, I heard her yelling. They made me keep her out … They made me!

FRUSTRATO

And that's when I came to visit you the first time. I was the replacement then, and I'm the replacement now.

HAROLD

What were you doing as a dog?

FRUSTRATO

I was a dog because that's what you needed at the time.

HAROLD

And now?

FRUSTRATO

And now I'm me, because this is what and who you need at this present moment.

HAROLD

I need a weirdo in a referee outfit with a painted face?

FRUSTRATO

You need a clown to bring back fun and joy into your life, someone with enough smarts to help you get rid of Lilly. That's me.

HAROLD

But they, them, and those said she could stay. She could stay with me. Lilly could stay with me, if I promised.

FRUSTRATO

If you promised what?

HAROLD

If I promised to be good. If I promised to listen to her and have discipline. They said she could stay. Lilly could stay if I had ... discipline.

FRUSTRATO

And have you had discipline, Harold?

HAROLD

I've tried, but the urges are strong, and I sometimes lose the battle.

FRUSTRATO

Yes, they know. They've been keeping an eye on you.

HAROLD

They! They! It's always they! They ... they ... THEY FUCKING!

(FRUSTRATO *uses his fingers to show that the words are in the wrong order. At first,* HAROLD *doesn't understand and imitates* FRUSTRATO'S *hand movements. Finally, he gets it.)*

HAROLD

Oh, right! Lilly is so much better at it than I am.

FRUSTRATO

I can help you with that too, Harold. I can teach you lots
of things when Lilly goes away.

HAROLD

Oh … but what about Lilly? What will happen to her?

FRUSTRATO

Who cares? She's a big girl. She can take care of herself.
Send her away. Don't worry about her. She won't miss
you.

HAROLD

She won't?

FRUSTRATO

Nah, she doesn't even like you. She only stays because
she enjoys giving you a headache. Send her away. Let her
give someone else a headache for a change.

HAROLD

Yeah, maybe she'll stay with Dr. Carney. Let *him* have a
headache now. (HAROLD *laughs.*) Soon he'll be coming
over here asking for *my* pills! (HAROLD *and* FRUSTRATO
laugh. HAROLD *catches himself and looks toward the
bedroom.*) Shhh …

FRUSTRATO

You see, you're growing already.

HAROLD

(Looking down at his crotch.) I am? I didn't think it showed.

(They laugh.)

FRUSTRATO

We're having fun, aren't we?

HAROLD

Yes, I know … I wish Lilly would like to have fun like this.

FRUSTRATO

Pfff, you can forget that. She's too uptight. You'll never have any fun as long as she's around. Get rid of her like I said and you'll kill two birds with one stone.

HAROLD

Two birds?

FRUSTRATO

Certainly. Don't you see? They, them, and those will be happy you've finally been able to dump Lilly, and you'll still have fun with me—on the QT, of course. We can do whatever we want. What do you say? You want to get started?

HAROLD

We're back to that again. Things are always going in circles when I talk with you.

FRUSTRATO

That's life. You can't escape the circles.

HAROLD

It seems I can't escape a lot of things.

FRUSTRATO

Circles are not something you want to avoid. The way I see it, you start out as nothing, and eventually you end up in the same place. Doesn't it make sense to head back around from the get-go? You're only going to wind up there anyway.

HAROLD

It seems futile. Why not travel in a straight line?

FRUSTRATO

A straight line, you say. Okay, Mr. Explorer, which way would you rather be going?

HAROLD

I don't know. North, I guess.

FRUSTRATO

Why north? Why not south?

HAROLD

I don't know, I—

FRUSTRATO

Or what about east? Why not pick east? Have you a problem with east?

HAROLD

Why no, I don't. You told me to pick a direction and—

FRUSTRATO

West. Ever been west?

HAROLD

No, I haven't. I suppose I could go west.

FRUSTRATO

It's too late now; you already chose north.

HAROLD

I don't know why I chose north; it was the first word that popped into my mind. There's nobody up north I want to see. I just said it, that's all.

FRUSTRATO

I shouldn't blame you. Your upbringing dictates your directional habits. I am disappointed, though. One day I'll ask that question and someone will say northeast, or southwest, or some other point on the compass that isn't on a cruciform. Wouldn't that be novel?

HAROLD

I'm certain it would be refreshing.

FRUSTRATO

Who am I kidding? It'll never happen. The compass points north, and it reflects the way people's minds point, too. But you just wait another three million years and guess what happens then?

HAROLD

I'm clueless.

FRUSTRATO

North becomes south and south becomes north! *(Rubbing his hands together.)* Isn't that delicious?

HAROLD

Get off it.

FRUSTRATO

It's true. Every 3 million years, the poles reverse themselves.

HAROLD

You're pulling my leg.

FRUSTRATO

It's been proven. It's in the rocks. Ah, but here is where the question lies: Does this transformation happen overnight? Or does it happen slowly? Will we wake up one morning and suddenly find that the compass is pointing south? Or does it happen slowly, over time, so that the compass points to all the directions between north and south as things begin to change?

HAROLD

That would certainly put a crimp in air traffic control's safety measures.

FRUSTRATO

More importantly, in which direction will it change?

HAROLD

What do you mean?

FRUSTRATO

Will the needle move clockwise or counter clockwise? Will it point north, and then northwest, then west, then southwest, then south? Or will it go in the opposite direction? North, northeast, east, southeast, south? These are perplexing questions.

HAROLD

I'll never sleep tonight.

FRUSTRATO

I haven't slept in weeks.

HAROLD

I wish I had chosen south.

FRUSTRATO

Be a compass, Harold. Move in circles.

HAROLD

There you go again—talking circles. When I move in circles, I never know where I am. I could be at the top, the bottom, or anywhere in between. *(Drawing a circle in the air with his finger.)* I never know if I'm on my way down or on my way back up. When I talk to Lilly, we move in one direction. Problem is, she always gets there before I do. She's very bright, you know.

FRUSTRATO

I wouldn't know. I don't know the woman. Nor do I care to.

HAROLD

Ever hear her use curse words?

FRUSTRATO

I've never had the pleasure.

HAROLD

She swears like a sailor—better than a sailor. She always gets it right. Amazing command of the language. It's remarkable. I'm in awe.

FRUSTRATO

It's a shame she has to go.

HAROLD

Who says?

FRUSTRATO

They say.

HAROLD

I'm sick of they, and I'm sick of them and those too. Why don't they, them, and those mind their own business.

FRUSTRATO

You are their business, and it's big business too. They make the decisions, and you must abide by them.

HAROLD

Well, I'm not happy.

FRUSTRATO

Happiness? Happiness? What does happiness have to do with anything?

HAROLD

One would like to be happy, don't you think?

FRUSTRATO

Happiness—pfff. It's fleeting at best. Happiness lasts a second or two and then it's over. Done. Kaput! Poof! It's a transitory emotion that escapes at a moment's notice. What's amazing is how people spend their entire lives vying for happiness, expecting it to last for longer periods of time than the sentiment permits. It's no wonder they never achieve it. There is something, however, that is a lot more infinite than happiness and so much more enjoyable. Do you know what that is?

HAROLD

A whoopie pie?

FRUSTRATO

Fun, Harold! Fun is the one thing that can go on forever. You can have fun from morning until night and never tire of it. You can have fun when you're three or three hundred years old. Fun knows no boundaries, no limits; there is no age requirement, and you don't need anyone else to have fun. You can have it alone or with others; it's your choice. You can have fun in the sun, fun in the shade, with clothes, without clothes (the better choice), in the desert, in the forest, in the light, in the dark, in the dark of the darkest dark where it's black of the blackest black and the blackness surrounds you to where you can't see two centimeters in front of your nose. You can still have fun there, in the black. Do you get it? Don't you get it? Am I the only one having fun here? *(Pauses. They stare at each other. After a moment.)* I'm waiting for a reply.

HAROLD

Oh, sorry. I thought that was a rhetorical question.

FRUSTRATO

No matter. What does matter is that fun is what's missing in your life, Harold, and together we can have it. But first, we need to rid ourselves of the bore sleeping in the next room. Otherwise our goose is cooked, the meat is overdone, and the fruit on the vine is rotten in the spine. So what do you say? Shall we do it?

HAROLD

I need time to think about this.

FRUSTRATO

What's to think about? You either want to have fun or you don't.

HAROLD

I *do* want to have fun … but does Lilly really have to go away?

FRUSTRATO

Of course she has to go! Don't you see? We won't have any fun if she stays here. She holds a gun to your head every time you want to do something fun. I can't imagine how you live like that. No! She'll have to go. Otherwise …

HAROLD

Otherwise what?

FRUSTRATO

Otherwise I will have to report to Dr. Carney, telling him you'd rather not have a replacement. I know he will not take too kindly to that attitude. I'm afraid I see lock-up in your future, and that would be a terrible shame, especially when you have such a sterling alternative.

HAROLD

Why would you do that?

FRUSTRATO

Because we, as humans, are taught from a very young age to turn upon ourselves.

HAROLD

So either Lilly goes or I get locked up, is that it?

FRUSTRATO

(Folding his arms across his chest.) Seems that way. You'll have to decide. You can either have fun *(pointing toward himself)* or the gun *(pointing toward the bedroom)*. Hey! I like the way that sounds. Don't you? Fun or the gun! *(Laughing.)* Fun or the gun! Fun or the gun!

HAROLD

(Laughing.) Fun or the gun! Fun or the gun!

(Together, they do a little dance and then follow each other as if in a conga line.)

HAROLD AND FRUSTRATO

FUN OR THE GUN! FUN OR THE GUN! FUN OR THE GUN! FUN OR THE GUN! FUN OR THE GUN! FUN OR THE GUN FUN OR THE GUN! FUN OR THE GUN!

LILLY

(Offstage.) HAROLD! GET IN HERE!

HAROLD

Uh-oh! Now we've done it! She sounds pissed.

FRUSTRATO

Good! Get in there and show her that you're in charge. Tell her you don't need her anymore. Let her know you've had enough of her bossing you around—telling you what you can and can't do. Now go. Tell her to get the hell out!

HAROLD

Oh … I don't think I can say it quite that way.

FRUSTRATO

Why not? Are you afraid?

HAROLD

No, I'm not afraid! I'm just … just …

FRUSTRATO

Just what ?

HAROLD

Just … well … yes, maybe I'm a little afraid.

FRUSTRATO

Hey, come on—it's only natural. You've been under her thumb for a long time. But don't worry; once you start on the road to independence, you'll find it gets easier by the minute.

HAROLD

She'll never agree to go.

FRUSTRATO

Well then, there are other ways.

HAROLD

You don't mean …

FRUSTRATO

Yes, I mean … Look, it's either you or her. *(In a gangster voice.)* Hey, we're talkin' survival here. You know what I mean, big guy?

HAROLD

What do I do if she doesn't want to leave?

FRUSTRATO

(In his own voice.) Then use this.

(FRUSTRATO *produces a switch blade knife that he pops open with a snap. He hands it to* HAROLD.)

FRUSTRATO

I've been saving it for a special occasion such as this.

HAROLD

(Staring at the knife.) Oh, I could never …

FRUSTRATO

Make it quick. She won't feel a thing.

HAROLD

You can't be serious.

FRUSTRATO

I've never been more serious in my entire life.

HAROLD

You're talking … murder!

FRUSTRATO

I'm talking survival. I'm talking freedom. More importantly, I'm talking fun.

HAROLD

But I'm not at all experienced.

FRUSTRATO

That's not what I hear.

HAROLD

(Pointing to the knife.) I'm talking about this!

FRUSTRATO

Oh, a simple affair, really. You simply point and push—hard.

HAROLD

But I've never …

FRUSTRATO

Not even once?

HAROLD

Not even once.

FRUSTRATO

Oh, I love a virgin. So this will be your first. Lucky guy.

HAROLD

I can't.

FRUSTRATO

Of course you can; it's easy.

HAROLD

If it's so easy then you do it. *(Offering to return the knife to* FRUSTRATO.*)*

FRUSTRATO

Hey, I can't do it! Don't you get it? We each must purge the devil from our *own* bosom. Now go on. Stiff upper lip. Get in there.

LILLY

(Offstage.) Harold! I told you to get in here!

HAROLD

Coming, Lilly. I'm just turning out the lights. *(To* FRUSTRATO.*)* Okay, I'm going in there. I'll try to convince her to leave so I don't have to use this … this … thing.

FRUSTRATO

It's show time, baby!

HAROLD

Okay, don't rush me, and don't interrupt us. Stay put. I'll do this my own way.

FRUSTRATO

Handle it any way you want. Only handle it.

(HAROLD *goes about the rooms shutting the lights.* FRUSTRATO *follows close behind, almost on top of him, pushing him, egging him on.* HAROLD *keeps turning back to* FRUSTRATO, *slapping at him, pushing him away. Finally,* HAROLD *walks toward the bedroom door.*)

HAROLD

Okay, now beat it!

FRUSTRATO

Have fun, you two. TTFN!

(HAROLD *composes himself, looks at the knife, puts it in the pocket of his robe, and shuts off the last light in the living room. The stage is black. He opens the bedroom door. He walks over to the lamp on his nightstand and turns it on.* LILLY *is sitting up in bed.* FRUSTRATO *is gone.*)

LILLY

What's going on, Harold? What were you doing out there?

HAROLD

Oh, nothing, Lilly. There's nothing going on.

LILLY

Don't lie to me, Harold. I heard you speaking with someone. Who were you talking to?

HAROLD

Well, if you must know … I was talking to the man *you* said didn't exist.

LILLY

You were out there a long time. What were you talking about?

HAROLD

Things.

LILLY

And what things might they be, Harold?

HAROLD

Well, if you must know … he is your replacement, Lilly.

LILLY

My replacement?

HAROLD

Yes, Lilly.

LILLY

I … I had no idea. I mean … already? I didn't think it would happen so soon. I thought we had more time.

HAROLD

So did I, Lilly. It appears we don't.

LILLY

So what did you tell him? Did you tell him that you don't want me to go? Did you tell him that we were happy together, that we *need* to be together? Did you mention that we are not at all happy with this arrangement? What did you tell him, Harold? Speak to me!

HAROLD

I explained all that and more, Lilly

LILLY

And? How did he react? What did he say? Surely he responded.

HAROLD

He said that if you didn't leave, they would lock me up again.

LILLY

I see … And what did you say? Did … did you plead
with him? Did you tell him that you—that we—would
be better? That we … we would try harder. Won't we,
Harold?

(HAROLD *walks around the bed to* LILLY's *side. His hand
is in his pocket. He walks behind* LILLY, *who sits facing
forward.*)

LILLY

We will, won't we? You and me, we'll try harder, right?
We'll do what they say. Right, Harold? We'll have
discipline, right?

HAROLD

Yes, Lilly.

LILLY

I know we can do better. We can, you know. You can
do anything you want if you put your mind to it. Isn't
that true, Harold?

HAROLD

Yes, Lilly, it's true.

LILLY

But then … I suppose … I suppose it's too late for that
… isn't that right, Harold?

119

HAROLD

Yes, Lilly, I'm afraid it's too late for that. But I still have one trick up my sleeve.

(HAROLD *removes the knife from his pocket. He looks at it. He looks at* LILLY, *who is still facing forward.* LILLY *and* HAROLD *both begin to cry.*)

LILLY

One trick left? Then I suppose you'd better use it, Harold. Don't you think so? Don't tell me about it. Just do it, okay? I know what must be done, and I understand, Harold … really, I do. Go ahead then. Just do it, okay?

(LILLY *closes her eyes.* HAROLD *wipes his eyes.*)

LILLY

Do it quickly, Harold? Okay?

HAROLD

Yes, Lilly, I will. I promise to do it quickly. (HAROLD *raises the knife above* LILLY *with both hands. He holds it in the air for a few seconds and then brings it down quickly, plunging the knife into his own chest. After a moment, he pulls it out and drops it to the floor. He staggers.)* Ohhh.

(LILLY *opens her eyes and brings her hands to her chest. She looks down at them as blood begins to stain her nightgown under her hands. She turns quickly toward* HAROLD.)

LILLY

Oh my God, Harold. What have you done? You've killed us!

HAROLD

No, Lilly. I've kept us together. Now, nothing will ever separate us or keep us apart.

LILLY

(Reaching out to HAROLD.*)* Come here, Harold. *(He staggers to her.)* Come up on the bed where I can feel you.

(HAROLD *gets on the bed.* LILLY *holds him and rests his head on her chest.*)

LILLY

Does it hurt, Harold?

HAROLD

No, Lilly. It doesn't hurt.

LILLY

What do you feel? I want to know. What does it feel like to die?

HAROLD

For the first time in a very long, long time, I feel … at peace.

(LILLY *and* HAROLD *hold each other for a while.*)

LILLY

I'm afraid, Harold. I'm afraid of where we're going.

HAROLD

I'm not, Lilly, because I'll be with you.

(LILLY *and* HAROLD *entwine. Fade to Black. Curtain falls.*)

The End